BARREN MOTHER
the True Story of God's Faithfulness to a Woman Who Felt Betrayed and Abandoned

Best Wishes,
Joanne

BARREN MOTHER
the True Story of God's Faithfulness to a Woman Who Felt Betrayed and Abandoned

By

JOANNE WILLIAMS

Scripture references are from
The Living Bible

ISBN: 1-58721-942-5

1stBooks - rev. 08/29/00

About The Book

Sometimes it takes failure or discouragement or an unexpected turn of events for us to realize that God not only knows us better than we know ourselves but He has a plan for us that we cannot comprehend in our limited humanness. He has the power to make us powerful but first He has to get our attention.

I had tunnel vision and a limited imagination about my future. Although I thought I was depending on God to lead me, the truth was that I wanted control and when things didn't go my way, and everything I planned fell apart, I felt betrayed and abandoned. Where was the God I trusted? He was waiting for me to hit rock bottom before I could realize He had different plans that were both frightening and exciting and would take me out of my comfort zone and into unknown territory. I had no choice but to totally surrender to His leading, one step at a time in order to emotionally survive. Often, I wondered if I would make it.

BARREN MOTHER takes me from a teenager who felt directed by God to be the mother of many children, to the young wife who made every effort to become pregnant and finally succumbed to the reality that she would never bear a child, to the woman who totally surrendered herself to God's will and the exciting life that followed. Had God shown a light far into my future, I would have crumbled under the frightening reality of the burdens I would have to bear. Fortunately, He promised me a "light unto my path," and, one step at a time, we walked a challenging path together.

The stories are true. Some of the names have been changed.

Thanks to a special group of friends
who knew me so many years ago and
shared the experiences recorded here.
Thanks to a select group of editors
who did not know me then so they could correct and
criticize and guide me without emotions
that come from "having been there."
Thanks to newspaper editors
Carol Bessey and Daryl Reinke
for thoughtful encouragement.
Above all, a posthumous thanks to editor,
Marg Green whose expertise brought the stories together
and made the years of writing and
rewriting worth it all.

viii

Prologue:

From the time I was a teenager, for whatever reason, I had a fascination with motherhood. This was before I dated, or even took an interest in boys, so it was not a romantic figment of my imagination. It was real, like an indication of God's direction for my life. No angel appeared with an announcement, nor can I say that God "spoke" to me. I only knew without a doubt that, regardless of my academic or career pursuits, motherhood was also to be my destiny and I sensed that God was preparing me to be the mother of many children.

Truthfully, it was a mystery. Why motherhood? And why by God's direction? My own family was no shining example. Certainly, both parents did their very best to instill into me those values they considered important. My father was creative and taught me to take risks in life without feeling defeated when they went sour. Mother balanced the relationship with practicality, patience, compassion, and probably a smattering of longsuffering. They both had many friends and taught me to be aware and concerned for the needs of others.

Our family was anything *but* religious. We called ourselves Christians but didn't attend church, read the Bible, or pray except for a memorized prayer they had me say at mealtime.

We were an average family, sometimes functional and sometimes very dysfunctional. Our secret (most families have at least one) was that my father had an alcohol problem he controlled during the day but succumbed to almost every evening. Mother's goal was to cover it up, by excuses if possible and denial if necessary. We were like a duck on a pond, appearing serene and peaceful but paddling mightily to maintain the image.

A young friend invited me to her Sunday School and that was the beginning of the beginning for me. I joined everything offered to my age group and, by the time I reached my early teens, understood the reality of a loving God who wanted only the best for me and would never leave me.

My life took a new direction as I recognized the power of prayer and saw where my parents were struggling with life's experiences on their own, facing one difficult problem after another with only each other to lean on, neither very steady. They were supportive of my new direction but not open to any changes themselves, so I began detaching from their struggles.

With excited anticipation, I accepted my high school sweetheart's marriage proposal, feeling confident that I knew what the future held. Years of child bearing. After all, isn't that how one gets to be the mother of many?

Two Become One

"We can make our plans, but the outcome is in God's hands"
(Proverbs 16:1).
Dear Friends,
How nice to see you at the wedding.
Thank you for the beautiful
Lazy Susan.
We will think fondly of you
every time we use it.
Regards,   Dave & Joanne

Nineteen forty nine was the year of the hammered aluminum wedding gift and we received seven Lazy Susans, all alike, with pears and leaves pounded around the tray. Fortunately, a local department store allowed us to exchange the surplus six for pots and pans that are still in use, over fifty years later, while the Lazy Susan disappeared long ago and has probably made the rounds of many a garage sale by now.

Dave was beginning his third of five years at the University of Minnesota and I worked in the office at Sears as the breadwinner while he completed his education. It had only been four years since the end of World War II and, as servicemen returned to set up housekeeping with their families, affordable housing was at a premium.

My gross salary of $180 a month limited us, but we finally rented a small apartment on the second floor of a house for $35 a month including utilities and excitedly spent a Saturday lugging our few pieces of furniture and wedding gifts up the narrow stairway. There was little storage and the Lazy Susan got shifted from table to corner to chair until it finally found a home under the bed.

Our landlady lived downstairs and was not a friendly sort. She was stingy and always acted suspicious, as if she were about to catch us in a evil act, like changing our light bulbs to stronger than 60 watts. We thought it was all quite hilarious and added to the thrill

1

of our new life together. To us, the tiny apartment was our castle and the landlady the Wicked Witch who lived outside the moat.

One privilege included in the rent was use of the washing machine in the basement, a dugout area under the house with a dirt floor. Makeshift shelves, lining the dirt walls, held toilet paper the landlady hoarded during the war. Apparently, she misjudged the ability of our Forces because the war had been over a few years and she still had at least a thousand rolls lining the makeshift shelves..

The old Maytag washing machine had a galvanized metal tub and a wringer (rollers) to squeeze out the water. After the load had agitated, I used a wooden stick to raise the clothes out of the hot, soapy, water and push them through the wringer. Then, I rinsed them by hand in another tub and pushed them through the wringer again.

Automatic washers and dryers had yet to be invented so, obviously, the Laundromat did not exist. I hung the clothes outside on a line to dry. It was September, still warm enough to require only a sweater, and the smell of burning leaves filled the air. Gentle Fall winds moved among the clothes and they dried quickly.

Then came winter. Minnesota winter. Hanging clothes outside no longer held the same glamour. Sandpaper stiff towels and frozen underwear were stacked in the basket like sheets of cardboard. Once inside, they thawed out limp and damp and had to be draped over furniture until dry. As the snow deepened, we strung clothesline from doorway to doorway and hung everything inside. The rooms became a maze of paths between sheets and shorts that took days to dry because the landlady controlled the heat and she stingily rationed it.

There was no thermostat. We had radiators that rarely got hot and sometimes we sat on them just to warm up. Entertaining guests looked like an Indian Pow-wow as we all sat around wrapped in blankets to keep warm. Thirty-five dollars a month got us a roof over our heads and Maytag privileges, little heat and no frills.

Although I knew something about cooking, it didn't take long to discover how little. We ate most of my mistakes because we were hungry and didn't have the money to give it a second try. One thing I remember having to throw out was the stewing hen I fried. It looked like something out of a magazine, browned to perfection. Then came the taste test. We couldn't get our teeth through the skin. The bird was tough as nails. Not one to be defeated, I filled a large cooking pot with water and popped the old hen in, crispy fried skin and all. After several hours at a ripping boil, nothing had changed. It was still as hard as a rock and I had no choice but to admit defeat.

This was but the beginning of many cooking struggles. Dave knew, without asking, that when I served toasted cheese sandwiches it was because the meal I planned was either in the garbage or buried somewhere.

Time For A Family

Children were not in our immediate plan but we both looked forward to parenthood and hoped for a large family. Secretly, we talked about an even dozen. Since we didn't have any at the time, a dozen sounded about right. After an intentionally childless period, we threw all caution to the wind and seriously set out to become pregnant.

Many of our friends were expecting their first child and we wanted to join the crowd. It seemed so simple; make love, miss a couple of periods, check with the doctor, and announce the good news. It worked for our friends and we assumed it would work for us.

Nothing happened. Month after month we waited, only to be disappointed. I often thought of the women of the Bible who were outcasts because they were "*barren*" and appreciated that I lived during a time in history when there were alternatives to bearing a child.

Even before marrying, Dave and I discussed this and decided that if, after exhausting every possibility, we could not become pregnant then adoption would be our option. We made a doctor appointment and began a series of procedures that proved successful for many other childless couples.

Those were the days prior to invetro fertilization and other high-tech processes. They did a procedure then called "blowing the woman's tubes." It was painfully uncomfortable but I willingly endured whatever it took to get this show on the road and begin a family. We also took into consideration that this was a stressful time for both of us with graduation approaching and companies coming on campus to interview students. The time was fast approaching for us to enter the real world.

5

Moving West

As much as we liked Minnesota and would miss our relatives and friends, we were anxious to live in a warmer climate. Neither of us had been beyond bordering states so the thought of moving far away held glamour and adventure.

The first three years of our marriage were financially strenuous but worth the struggle. Dave graduated with honors and we each took pride in our contribution to that goal. A California firm hired him for the whopping salary of $330 a month and we felt well on the road to financial success.

We sold our 1941 Oldsmobile Coupe and upgraded to a 1948 Hudson that carried us, and our worldly goods, west. What a car! Sleek and sporty with a dashboard full of lights. Lights for everything. When something was low, a warning light sent out it's message, "Sweetheart, I'm in a little need here." Why it never warned us when we were in town and near qualified help, I can't guess but, somewhere in the desert between Minnesota and California, a light gave its SOS and I got nervous. It seemed to say to me, "Hey, stupid, if you kept your eyes on the gauges you would have noticed, miles back, that I am running a little low on energy here."

Dave hadn't figured out all the dashboard signals yet so he stopped the car, raised the hood, and checked everything he knew how to but the light persisted. My nervous chatter didn't help and, since the source was a mystery, Dave asked me to cover the light with my foot so I wouldn't be bothered by it. Each time I moved my foot and peeked, the light peeked back. "You have to do something!" I nervously nagged. Once again, he stopped the car and raised the hood. After a short time, he hopped back behind the wheel and, when he turned on the key, the light remained off. What a relief! What a man! It wasn't until we arrived in California that he confessed he got the light to turn off by disconnecting it.

If At First You Don't Succeed

Once settled in an apartment, we resumed medical assistance to become pregnant and there followed many procedures, all with no success. We were discouraged and desperate but tried to maintain a sense of hope (and humor) through it all.

Looking back, I can't help but smile but, at the time, it was a heavy burden. I recorded my temperature each morning so the doctor could determine when I ovulated. At that magic moment, we were advised by the doctor to have intercourse with a special condom that Dave then, lovingly, tucked under his armpit to keep the sperm warm while he rushed it and me to the hospital where she somehow inserted the sperm into whatever my "right part" was and sent me home to spend the next 24 hours on my back with hips elevated on pillows.

When this procedure proved unsuccessful, she gave me the option of having insemination with someone else's sperm, noting that many bright, talented, healthy medical students sold their sperm to a Bank where it was frozen until needed. I chose not to accept that offer. If Dave and I could not produce a child together then we would adopt one together. What a long way medical science has come in assisting couples to become pregnant now. Mix a sperm and an egg in a saucer and Voila, a baby for many anxious couples.

I mentioned that my doctor was a woman - quite unusual for specialists then and she was of little comfort to my dilemma since she, herself, popped babies out like jellybeans and went back to work the next week. In fact, she had a baby while I was her patient and I read in the paper that it arrived so fast, she delivered it herself on the kitchen floor.

Disappointing News

"I have no hope except in you"
(Psalms 25:5b).

The weeks and months turned into a year, and then another year with no specific reason why I could not become pregnant. Finally, the dreaded day came when the doctor called us in and suggested that perhaps we should consider adoption. It was a sad moment for us both and I confess that I tear up at the memory.

I must thank my Mother for her valuable insight. In response to my letter with the devastating news, she wrote back, "I am truly sorry that you cannot have your own children. I looked forward to it, also. However, let me remind you that many of your friends have husbands who are fighting in Korea at this very moment. Some of them will be injured and others will not return at all. You have each other and you are together. You have much to be thankful for and I know that, somehow, you will manage to overcome this sad moment and find happiness in your future."

She was right, of course, but I felt too "*barren*" to think about anything but the loss of an experience I had anticipated since my teens. Had God gone back on a promise? What made me think it was a promise at all? Was this business about becoming the mother of many some figment of my imagination?

I missed my parents and wanted to move back to Minnesota but it was costly. The few possessions we packed into the Hudson had multiplied into what could now be considered "much worldly goods." Dave recognized how disappointed and sad I was about our medical status, and how I longed for the comfort of my mother, so he agreed to move back if we could find the financial resources.

"Dear Dad," I wrote, "With all the testing we've been through, and now this discouraging news, I feel like I need to be closer to you and Mom. Dave has agreed to move back if you are willing to loan us the money." I went on to assure him that we would repay on a regular basis, with interest, and asked how he felt about it.

11

His reply arrived in a few days. "I will be glad to send you the money in one year," he wrote. "My advice is to give anything a year, whether it is a move, a job, or any important change." He went on to say that it often takes time to feel comfortable in these situations and a year should tell us, one way or the other, if change is the best solution. What sage advice! And, he was speaking to his only child, the apple of his eye. He put my needs before his own and it was all the advice we needed.

Within the next year we took two trips back to Minnesota and realized that our place was in California. With two salaries, we saved enough for the down payment on a two bedroom house, one for us and one for the nursery.

Do We Qualify?

Our focus now was investigating adoption possibilities. Some friends had adopted through a lawyer, only to have the birth mother return to claim the child before the adoption was final. It was such a traumatic experience for their family, we decided to opt for a County Agency adoption which offered better security. Upon contacting them, their enthusiasm renewed our spirits and it sounded like the possibility of getting a child was eminent. Actually, it was still years away.

We tried to relax as we waited and planned, no longer for an even dozen but, perhaps, for four. Weeks and months passed with an occasional visit from a social worker.

"Let's talk about finances," the worker smiled as she pulled a pad and pencil from her briefcase. "Do you own any stock?" "No." "Bonds or Mutual Funds?" "No." We were young, buying our first home, which had less than 1,000 square feet and cost under $10,000, and there was little left over after the basic bills. I wondered if we were meeting the Agency's financial criteria. Surely they observed that we were good managers and would work hard to provide the proper home environment for any child.

The Workers were cordial and encouraging. After about two years, the visits became less frequent and we were told that, when they felt the right baby was available, we would be contacted. At first, I hesitated leaving the house for fear I would miss THE call. Somehow, I felt that the Agency might go down their list and pick the next name if we were not home. I knew better but I was so anxious. As the days and weeks passed, I returned to a more normal routine and did my best to relax and wait patiently.

In the meantime, I missed a menstrual period and, upon visiting our family physician, was told I was probably pregnant. There seemed to be some concern but, after the next month, the doctor was reasonably certain. We couldn't have been more thrilled and immediately called our families and announced the good news to the neighborhood.

God hadn't disappointed me, after all. For the next two weeks, I was in a happy stupor. I was going to have a baby. Maybe we could boost that number back up from four to at least six.

A Dream Shattered

"I scream for help and no one hears me.
I shriek, but get no justice"
(Job 19:7-8).

The abdominal pains began in the night and became increasingly severe. I decided not to tell Dave. Having never been pregnant, I thought the pains might be normal but, by morning, they had become progressively worse so I made an emergency visit to the doctor. After a pelvic exam, he called a specialist in the next city who agreed to see me as soon as I could get there.

The obstetrician examined me while a secretary who sat nearby took his dictation. As I listened, it became apparent that I was not, and never had been, pregnant. A large cyst was growing on one of my ovaries and this is where the blood from my menses had collected. This was on a Friday and surgery was scheduled for the following Monday. The drive home seemed to take forever and, once again, my dreams were shattered. Dave had been so pleased about our having a baby and now I would tell him it was not to be.

As I sobbed over the phone, he listened and reminded me that we didn't tell the Agency about the pregnancy, in case there was some complication such as this, and we were still high on their list of prospective adoptive parents. I hung the phone up and thanked God for the comfort of an understanding husband. Even though I knew there was nothing I could have done to prevent this turn of events, somehow I felt responsible.

During the surgery, the cyst, an ovary, and my appendix were removed and the doctor performed an exploratory that revealed endometriosis, a condition in the lining of the uterus. Perhaps that interfered with a pregnancy. All I wanted was to recover as rapidly as possible in case an adoptable baby became available.

My body did a better job of healing than my mind. While in the hospital, my roommate died and, since the facility was too crowded to move her, we remained roommates for several hours. When the funeral director finally arrived, he bagged her and

15

removed her on a dolly, turning as he left to wish me good luck. By that time, I needed more than luck. I needed someone to tell me I wasn't going to die, too. A cloud of gloom hovered over me and, even after leaving the hospital, I felt depressed and sad and cried at the drop of a hat. I didn't tell my doctor because my condition was not physical and I couldn't express how I felt mentally. When there still was no improvement after a couple of weeks, I finally phoned my doctor and he scolded me for waiting so long and assured me that this was a normal reaction to having an ovary removed, which interrupts the hormone balance. How I wished he had indicated that possibility before the surgery. I made an appointment to see him that day and, soon after I began taking the prescribed hormone pills, I felt better than I had in months. It was July of 1954.

Answered Prayer

"Then he placed a little child among them;
and taking the child in his arms he said to them,
Anyone who welcomes a little child like this in my name
is welcoming me, and anyone who welcomes me
is welcoming my Father who sent me!"
(Mark 9:36-37).

Four months passed. About nine o'clock on a November morning, the phone rang. I was finishing the breakfast dishes and grabbed a towel. "Good morning, Joanne," the soft female voice said. "This is the County Adoption Agency." I clutched the phone and answered her greeting. Was she calling to make an appointment for another home visit? Could this possibly be THE call?

"We have a beautiful baby girl here that we think would be just right for you and your husband. She's five weeks old with light brown, almost blonde, hair and big blue eyes. Can you come down tomorrow morning at ten to see her?" Trembling with joy, I assured her we would be there and after hanging up the phone I raised my grateful hands to heaven and cried, "Thank you Lord, thank you Lord, thank you Lord," over and over through my tears. The long, lonely wait was coming to an end. God did have a plan for me after all. I called Dave.

We arrived at the agency well before ten the next morning. The waiting area was austere and void of anything that added beauty and charm. Folding chairs lined the walls. We sat down and waited a short while before the social worker and another woman, carrying a small bundle wrapped in a knit blanket, entered and greeted us warmly.

The stranger, apparently a foster mother, lovingly lowered her arms to mine and laid the Gift in them. I pulled back the blanket and found myself holding the loveliest creature I had ever seen. She was soft and pink with what little hair she had coaxed into one curl on top. Her blue eyes were so big it reminded me of a newly hatched bird. For the next few moments, Dave and I were speechless and when words finally came, they were in a whisper as if a noise might break the spell and make the magic moment disappear.

After some discussion, the social worker told us it was Agency policy to have the prospective parents go home and decide if it was truly their intent to adopt this child. We could return the following day and take her home. Obviously we wanted her, but we graciously obeyed and spent another restless night talking and planning. No longer a couple, we were now a family. The following day we brought our daughter home and named her Diane Marie. The next day, most appropriately, was Thanksgiving Day, 1954.

She Arrived Without Instructions

One day I didn't have a baby and the next day I did. Now what? "How To" books about parenting were still in their author's minds. Fathers did not attend the birth or participate much in the care of infants. They worked to provide for the family needs while mother stayed home and managed the children. Phrases like "strong willed child" or "terrible twos" had not been coined. Baby made three and our life style went topsy-turvy until we could establish a new routine.

Neither of our families lived close by but we had helpful, and some not-so-helpful, friends and neighbors who were like family and never at a loss for advice. "Let her cry. It's good for the lungs." "Phew! What have you been feeding her?" "You still get up with her in the night?" I vowed not to compare Diane with other children but other parents did not make that easy. Why is it that the neighbor kid slept through the night before she left the hospital and was potty trained after one brief lesson?

Like most first mothers, I wanted very much to be perfect. After the first child, most parents stop trying because we learn that perfection is impossible. Some wise guru once said that the first child grows up in spite of us and I apologetically agree.

One of my favorite and most respected friends, the mother of a neighbor, was flying in from out of state and I wanted to impress her with my mothering skills. The neighbor invited me to bring Diane over for an afternoon visit so I planned it after her nap, insuring her alertness and good behavior. From her frilly petticoat and sox to the pink pleated dress to the patent leather shoes with a strap and button, she was one cute little girl.

Of course, my friend's mother made a fuss over her and we settled in for a nice chat while Diane sat quietly on my lap. Finally, this friend I wanted so much to impress asked, "Joanne, why do you have her shoes on the wrong feet?" I looked down and, sure enough, those toes were pointing out instead of in. As embarrassed as I was, this turn of events was a blessing in disguise because I recognized that the truth was out. I was not a perfect mother and both Diane and I were free from having to reach for impossible goals and unrealistic expectations.

God is good, and gentle, as He teaches us life's little lessons. He and I had a quiet conversation, then and there, and I said, "Thanks" on behalf of both of us.

The adoption became final within the first year and it was a day of joyous relief for Dave and me because we knew there would be less chance of a natural parent showing up at our door unexpectedly and claiming their child. Until then, I had a nagging little fear every time the phone or doorbell rang. The thought of losing Diane was almost paralyzing. With the final papers in hand, we felt confident about applying for a second child.

Although Diane was matched to our appearance, we were informed that a much quicker adoption was possible if we were willing to take a physically handicapped or mixed race child, which we agreed to consider. Once again, the possibility of a large family sounded encouraging and our name went on the waiting list. Had we remained with that Agency, our dream may have become a reality but, shortly after celebrating Diane's second birthday, Dave was transferred with his company and our family moved.

Although it was a job promotion with an exciting future, leaving our close knit neighborhood was difficult because these people had become our extended family. They rejoiced when we thought we were pregnant, agonized over the news that there was no baby, upheld us through my surgery and recovery and shared the joy of Diane's adoption as if she belonged to them, also. Now, it was time to leave the comfort of this relationship and move on.

The best offer on the sale of our house included our taking a used Cadillac as part of the down payment. It was big, plush, and totally out of character for us considering our other vehicle was a beat up old pickup truck. We made a strange looking little parade, Diane in her car seat beside me in the Cadillac and Dave following closely behind in the pickup, as we pulled away from the neighborhood, onto the freeway and north to a new life.

One of the most difficult ties to break was with the Adoption Agency because we knew they had our history, that the preliminaries were already behind us, and the possibility of more adoptions was real. However, the county we were moving to also had an Agency and we assumed it must be similar to the one we were leaving. All they needed to do was send for our records and continue from there. How naive and unprepared we were for the turn of events ahead.

"We Take Trades"

Getting settled took time; first a small apartment, then a rented house, and finally a purchased home. The latter was in a new development, close to shopping and a church we attended. Even Dave's drive to work was pleasant. At first, we didn't consider the purchase of that house seriously because the down payment was beyond our budget but, having looked for months, I knew this house was the best value on the market and decided to approach the possibility creatively.

I telephoned ahead for an appointment and the eager salesman was waiting at the open door when I pulled up to the model home. After exchanging a few pleasantries, I pointed to the giant banner over the entrance to the subdivision. It read, WE TAKE TRADES. "There's my trade," I said, pointing to the Cadillac. After a healthy laugh, he explained that I misunderstood the banner which meant that they take other houses in trade for full or partial down payment on these homes.

Not one to be easily discouraged, I led him to the car and, while he slid the key into the ignition, I slid into the passenger seat and the two of us went for a "spin." The final paperwork may have looked unusual but I left holding a contract for the trade. The salesman got the car of his dreams and we got the house of ours.

Dreams Unfulfilled

In the meantime, we initiated adoption proceedings by beginning the interview process. We were comforted by the thought that all we needed was time for the Agency to process our application, make the necessary home visits, and our next adoption would be eminent. Wrong!

After a few visits to the Agency office, we took the routine physicals, as we had done before. Dave had a heart condition resulting from rheumatic fever as a child. He made no effort to conceal that information and had taken physicals for employment and our previous adoption with no problem but the doctor at this Agency informed us that we could not be candidates for an adoption, ever, because of this condition.

As grateful as I was to have Diane, my world crumbled as I faced the reality that I would never be the mother of many children. Where was God in all this confusion? Had I misunderstood His intention for me? I felt fragile, abandoned, and forgotten.

Diane lacked companionship her age. We were only the second home owners to move into the development and, until more homes were completed and occupied, Diane had no playmates except Mitzi, our German Shepard. We enrolled Diane in a local preschool where she spent weekday mornings. Upon her return home I would ask how the morning went. "Fine," was the simple reply. "What did you do today," I continued. "Nothing." Then, she and the dog would go into the closet where she shared the events of the day. Mitzi was a large dog and when the two of them squeezed into the closet, along with the clothes and toys that belonged there, it was "togetherness" in the purest form. After some time, they would both emerge, smelling like dog. Mitzi filled a void until other children moved in around us.

Dave enjoyed Diane and spent as much time as possible with her. As his responsibilities increased at work, so did his salary and we were able to provide Diane with every creature comfort. She had so many clothes, I could hardly stuff them into the dresser drawers and closet. There was enough for five children.

I was also making another mistake. Instead of enjoying Diane for the moment, for whatever little things she did or said, I was planning her future. Not just her immediate future. I was thinking about where she would attend college. Remember now, we are dealing with a three year old. I needed someone else to share my attention with. There was an empty place inside of me that could only be filled by more children.

God's Plan, Not Mine

"Lord, I lift my hands to heaven and
implore your help. O, listen to my cry"
(Psalms 28:2).

Events couldn't occur fast enough for me. I had my own agenda and wanted life to pick up some speed and move, move, move. One day, when I felt particularly low, I was preparing lunch and turned on the radio to catch the noon news. Suddenly, a depression overwhelmed me and I dissolved into tears as my body began to shake and lower to the floor. I cried out loud, "Lord, help me! What do you want of me? Am I missing something? Misinterpreting something? I want to serve you, to please you, but everywhere I turn there seems to be a closed door. Speak to me in a way I can understand, Lord."

The sobbing quieted, the trembling ceased, and I lay on the floor in total exhaustion. I listened as a radio announcer finished his news segment and then an unusual commercial followed. It was an appeal from the local County Foster Parenting Program to anyone willing to share their home with children who were removed from their own homes because of abuse or neglect or circumstances that rendered the natural parent unable to attend to the child's daily needs.

Could this be God's way of speaking to me? If so, it certainly was an immediate response to my plea, and in a way I could understand. I almost laughed as I pulled myself up to a chair and reached for the telephone to call Dave at work. He agreed that it sounded challenging and would provide companionship for Diane while helping another child. My next call was to the County Welfare Department.

"Here we go again!" I thought. "Back to square one with applications, social workers, home visits, and waiting." This time, I was wrong. The process was faster and less involved and, within a month, we were gifted with our first two of fourteen foster children.

27

It was the beginning of an education that took me out of my comfort zone where I always had enough food and clothes, not just a roof over my head but a nice place to live, and people around me whom I trusted to love and protect me. Until now, I naively prided myself on understanding human nature but I was soon to learn how pampered I had been. No past experience prepared me for what lay ahead.

Precious Little Strangers

"Don't forget to be kind to strangers,
for some who have done this have entertained
angels without realizing it"
(Hebrews 13:2).

Ricky, age nine, and his seven year old half-sister, Maryann, shared the same mother. They were two of four children with an older brother in another foster home and a two year old sister at home with the mother. The social worker did not give me any information about Rickys natural father and, in conversation, both children called Maryann's father "Daddy." Ricky had sandy colored hair and freckles across the bridge of his nose. He was quiet, thoughtful, and mellow.

Maryann was the talker. She had bright red hair that was a tangle of tight natural curls and her cheeks and nose were covered with freckles. Cautiously, they got out of the County car and the social worker ushered them inside the house. She didn't have to help them with their belongings for each child carried one paper grocery bag that held not only their clothes but their toys, also.

The social worker stayed long enough for them to become acquainted with the house and with me. Then she left, making arrangements to phone the next day for an update. Diane cautiously held my hand as we ushered the children through the house. For the first time, she would be sharing her room and her closet and her possessions, so many possessions compared to the few little things in Maryann's paper bag.

It was a beautifully sunny day, a happy day for me. After enjoying cookies and milk, we went outside to meet the dog. She was friendly but so large she almost knocked the children over, which would not have been difficult. Ricky wore short pants and his knees were so knobby, they seemed too big for his legs. Mitzi welcomed both children by rubbing against them and the bonding began.

29

"I want to give you each an allowance, at the end of the week, for some small jobs you can help me with," I said. Both children showed interest. "Ricky, your job will be to keep the back yard cleaned of dog dirt." Silence. Then, he looked at me soberly and said, "OK."

Let me say here that the dog was big and she pooped big and everywhere in the back yard. While Ricky was quiet and obliging, Maryann spoke her mind whenever and wherever she considered it appropriate. "That was his job at our last foster home, too," she said. I knew this was the fifth foster home these children had been in and, although I didn't know the circumstances, I suddenly felt that Ricky was a boy with a broken spirit. Perhaps he had been mistreated somewhere along the line and now he was reduced to a little robot. I also realized that I was giving him a job I hated and wanted to get out of. God was, once again, gently making me aware of my misguided intentions and this, like putting Diane's shoes on the wrong feet, was one more learning experience.

"Well," I said, "it sounds like you know how to do that already, Ricky, so why don't I clean up after the dog and find you another job?" He showed little expression but I could tell he wasn't disappointed. That experience led me to question my motives from then on and, if the job was not a desirable one, I offered to share it.

We cleaned their rooms and did the dishes and prepared school lunches together and we talked and laughed and sang together as they, little by little, day by day, inched their way into our routine and into our hearts.

The first night the children were with us, I asked if they knew anything about prayer. "Oh yes," Ricky eagerly replied, "I know the Lord's Prayer," and he began, "Our father, who art in heaven, Hollywood be thy name." I knew my work was cut out for me.

I suggested they pray for anyone they wanted to and believe that God heard them and would answer their prayer. Maryann was creative each night with a different sentence prayer but Ricky always said the same thing, "Dear God, please help my Daddy to be kind to others." He never deviated.

*"And if God provides clothing for the flowers
that are here today and gone tomorrow,
don't you suppose that he will provide
clothing for you, you doubters?"
(Luke 12:28).*

These two new additions to our family taught me a lot about what is really important. As I looked at Diane's closet and dresser drawers, crammed so full I could hardly close them, and I thought of the two grocery bags that held our new children's possessions, my priorities began to change.

It didn't take me long to realize that a child does not need a wardrobe of clothing but just enough for the next few days, and the outfits don't need to be color coordinated, just clean. I also learned to appreciate the blessings of the day, and that included my husband and children.

Planning for Diane's college, fifteen years away, seemed unrealistic when these children were only ours for today, maybe tomorrow or the next week or month or year. One thing was certain. At some time, they would be taken from us. As we accepted this reality, we realized that our time with Diane was also precious, and momentary. What a happy discovery! Dave and I made every effort to enjoy them all and help Ricky and Maryann to learn new skills and become as independent as possible, considering their age.

Dave did the outdoor things, like getting parts at a local auction yard and putting together bikes. My job was to take care of their more personal needs and educate them to care for themselves and each other should they leave us for less desirable circumstances.

They learned how to read a thermometer and call for emergency help and how to cook simple foods that were nourishing. I taught them about good dental care and general health.

The teeth thing became an issue when, shortly after they arrived, Maryann complained of a toothache. When I asked if she could tell me which tooth bothered her, she said, "The black one." I hesitated looking, uncertain of what I might find, and my fears were realized in a molar that was decayed down to the gum line. All

31

that showed was black. "How could this happen to innocent children who depend on others for their welfare?" I thought. I was angry at her mother, at the foster care system, and anything else that allowed such neglect. We trotted to the dentist that very afternoon and the remainder of the tooth was extracted.

There were many opportunities to teach Ricky and Maryann about life, relationships, and making choices but the most important issue to me was that they learn how much God loved them and would always be with them. No matter how many physical changes they were forced to make, I felt that they needed to know God went along and was always available to them through prayer.

We spent time, every night before bedtime, reading and talking. As the weeks passed, Ricky developed a trust that allowed him to share some of his feelings, and some of his past experiences, with me. He still had not altered his bedtime prayer for his Daddy to be kind.

He told me that, when his Daddy was angry with him and his older brother, he hung them from large hooks on the wall. "Am I hearing right?" I thought. Little children hanging from hooks? Our society treats hardened criminals more humanely. The boys were helpless against this tyrannical father. He also beat them with his belt and punished them so severely one time that the belt buckle broke off. "But it was an old belt," Ricky added, almost defending the man.

Finally, the abuse became so unbearable that, after a particularly severe punishment, the boys decided to run away. They each had less than a dollar in change and spent it on ice cream. Night time came and they had no where to go and not even a sweater to keep them warm. They huddled together on the bank of a local river and, when they got hungry, they ate grass. After a couple days without food or adequate clothing, they stopped a police car and asked for help. That led to an investigation of the home and removal of Maryann, also.

Apparently, it was felt that the mother could keep the youngest child but I often questioned that decision because, when she came to pick up Ricky and Maryann for visits, the youngster looked malnourished and dirty, with large clumps of hair missing.

32

There was no visible father figure but always a man for transportation to and from our home. Ricky spoke of the taxi drivers who spent the night and "hurt" his mother. We suspected these to be sexual partners and not abusers.

"You should defend those who cannot help themselves,
Yes, speak up for the poor and needy
and see that they get justice"
(Proverbs 31:8-9).

Ricky loved his mother and felt responsible for helping her. The first visit away from us, she took his allowance. It was so little, I wondered what she could buy with it but he let her have it willingly. When he told me, I suggested he leave his allowance at our house and, if he saw that his mother was in real need, I would let the social worker know. I didn't want to reveal my anger at his mother for taking his hard earned fifty cents because he had enough issues to deal with for a nine year old, but I also knew that he needed an advocate. If his mother had real financial needs that were not being met, I was willing to be an advocate for her also but, from what I observed, she could manage without his half dollar allowance.

Maryann joined the Brownies and Ricky became a Cub Scout. They loved the social involvement and opportunity to earn badges. And, they loved school. One of their teachers had known them from a previous school and couldn't believe it was the same children. She said they each showed remarkable improvement, socially and scholastically. A new experience for them was Sunday School.

It was a particularly proud Sunday when Ricky, along with the other fourth graders, received a Bible at the end of the school year. He proudly walked to the front of the church when his name was called, shook hands with the pastor, and held the Bible as if it were a prized possession. Finally, something he had earned to call his very own. I hoped that, when the time came to leave us, the Bible

33

would be a companion and reminder not only of God's love but our love also.

Answered Prayer

"All that's required is that you
really believe and have no doubt"
(Mark 11:23b).

Maryann was enthusiastic about bedtime prayer and became more creative and expressive each evening. As young as Diane was, she emulated Maryann in her own three year old way. Ricky stuck to the same prayer, even the same words night after night, "Help my Daddy to be kind to others."

We had many good opportunities to talk about trusting God and I felt that Ricky had no other choice because I was told his father had left the area and not been heard from for some time. I am almost ashamed to say that I hoped prayer would help. I did not feel as convincing as I sounded but Ricky sincerely believed it and trusted that, wherever his father was, God was changing him.

One day, I got an unexpected phone call from the social worker. She said that the children's father was visiting in town and wanted to see them. She would be by on Saturday morning to pick them up and I was welcome to ride along if I wished. "No thanks," I thought. I was afraid of the guy, even though we had never met, but then I realized what a coward I was being. The children HAD to go. No choice. The least I could do was to be there to support them.

When I told them, Maryann seemed pleased and excited. This surprised me because the social worker told me that they suspected the father of sexually molesting her when she was about five years old. Although she never verified that, she did tell me her Daddy did some things to her that were not nice. Ricky was visibly shaken at the thought of being near his Daddy. I promised to be there beside him and assured him that the social worker would not arrange any meeting that was harmful to either of the children.

Saturday morning arrived and so did the social worker. Maryann jumped into the front seat and chattered all the way, a long drive to another part of the city. Ricky didn't utter a word for

35

the entire trip as the two of us sat, silently, in the back seat. We pulled up in front of a small bungalow in a run down neighborhood and, after a brief wait, the father answered our knock at the door.

I don't know what I expected but this man was HUGE, well over six feet and heavy set. Instantly, I thought of how frightening it must have been for a little boy to have this hulk of a man beating on him with a belt and hanging him from a hook on the wall. To my surprise, he was soft spoken and quietly invited us in, motioning for us to sit down. Maryann remained beside him and eventually sat on his lap. Ricky, on the other hand, stood as far across the room as he could and remained silent.

In a kind voice, the father inquired of the children about their life and what was happening to them now. They told him about our house and family, school and Scouts, Sunday School and Mitzi. Maryann elaborated in a continuous chatter that included animated gestures. Ricky stuck to short, quiet answers. The conversation went on for almost an hour before the social worker suggested it was time to leave. I was ready, although the visit had been much different and more enjoyable than I expected.

This man puzzled me and it was clear that he was not the man the children remembered. Finally, just before we left, Ricky walked across the room and put his arms around the big man's neck and said, "I can hardly believe this is really you," and he kissed his Daddy on the cheek. It was a profound moment that will forever be etched in my memory because it was a kiss of forgiveness and absolution by a loving son and the gentle holding hug of a repentant father.

God revealed his love to Ricky by allowing him to see a father who had been changed through the power of prayer. Ricky never doubted it. Only I did. Surely this was what Jesus referred to when he admonished us to have the faith of a child and I was genuinely humbled. Both Ricky and I had anticipated a frightening experience on the drive over and, instead, we were treated to a miracle.

There was not much conversation, even from Maryann, on the way home. Each of us was in a reflective mood but I think Ricky felt the most at peace because he had believed and now he experienced the personal power of prayer.

36

Losing Our First Foster Children

When I answered the phone, a few weeks later, it was the call I had dreaded. The social worker explained that the children's mother was moving to another city, some distance away, and she wanted the children near her. They would move within the month. "Why?" I pondered. "Why is this mother showing a sudden interest when, often, she didn't show up for arranged visits or follow through with plans and promises?" "Why, God? Why?" Dave and Diane and I wanted so much for Ricky and Maryann to stay and remain part of our family.

We offered to transport them regularly to visit their mother if she allowed them to remain with us. This would have meant a big sacrifice but we were willing to do anything to keep our little "makeshift" family together. Their mother refused. When the school teachers heard about it, they we so upset, they attempted to intervene by writing to the Governor of our state, telling him of the remarkable social and scholastic advances these children had made while in our care. The Governor refused to become involved.

Because we loved the children and were genuinely concerned about their welfare, we offered to adopt them but were told that foster children were *not* adoptable and we should *never* consider that option again, with any foster child. Also, the Agency felt that, once the children left our home, we should have no further contact with them because it might be difficult for them to adjust to their new surroundings. How could the Agency possibly expect us to let the children vanish, as if our relationship never existed?

On the designated day, the social worker parked in our driveway and opened all the doors and the trunk of her car. She was as hurt as the rest of us but we understood that she had no choice and I sensed her frustration. This had been a good foster home placement and she took pride in the time and effort put into it. No one knew what lay ahead but every one of us feared that it would be disappointing.

Where her car easily held the two paper bags the children carried when they arrived at our home, she now pondered how to fit everything in. There were boxes of toys and clothing, two bikes and a Bible. Before the children left, we took a moment together and prayed. I reminded them that God was wherever they were and they had but to call upon Him.

To say that our parting was painful would be inadequate. I felt ripped apart This was our first experience at fostering children and I had no idea how much it would hurt when they left us. Had I known their next home would be a safe, secure, loving one, it might have eased the agonizing pain.

We never saw or heard from Ricky or Maryann again. The social worker informed us that there were no foster homes where their mother moved, so they were institutionalized.

Filling the Void

The loss created a huge vacuum in our home. No Maryann to be silly with. No Ricky to be serious with. No one for Diane to play with or argue with or share with. She must have had some concern about the reason for their leaving because she became the "perfect kid." After a couple days of this unusual behavior, she said, "I have to be real good, don't I Mommy, or I will have to leave, too." I assured her that, no matter how good or bad she was, she could stay forever. Knowing that helped us both.

Perhaps it was good that we had time without the added responsibility of other children because Diane began to display some unusual physical disorders on her left side. They came on slowly but finally developed a pattern we recognized as not normal.

Her left foot turned in and required an orthopedic correction with special shoes. Her left eye wandered out, particularly when she was tired, and required numerous visits to an ophthalmologist and a series of exercises we did at home. She wore a patch over the weak eye so it would track with the strong one. Her left kidney malfunctioned, allowing urine to back up into it instead of expelling. This is called Reflux and it resulted in urine infection and high fever which landed her in the hospital for treatment under anesthetic, followed by weekly visits to a urologist.

Did she enjoy the peace and solitude of being the only child again? Absolutely not! She was miserable and lonely. She missed the company and excitement of other children in the house. "Get some more kids in here," she said one night. "I need some more kids!" I called the Agency and told them we were ready for another child or two, expecting active little companions for Diane. The Agency had other plans.

"We have a newborn baby who needs foster care," the social worker said. That was exciting news. Dave and I both loved babies and, although she might not be a companion Diane's age, she would be fun for Diane to be with and help care for. Besides, babies grow fast and develop abilities to walk and talk and play. I imagined her, before long, following Diane around the house.

Then, as I held the phone with one hand and began writing information with the other, I realized that this was no ordinary baby. This was a child with special needs and we were to try and fill them.

Kathy

*"O God, you have declared me
perfect in your eyes"
(Psalms 4:1).*

Kathy looked normal. In fact, the first day we had her, I must
have been in denial. I was told that she could not be released for
adoption because of complications during the birth process but I
saw nothing wrong. When the pediatrician's nurse called to see
how I was doing, I told her, "There's nothing wrong with this baby.
She's perfectly normal." After a long silence, the nurse said,
"Joanne, that baby is severely brain damaged from lack of oxygen
during birth."

How could I not have noticed? She was limp and unable to
move her arms or legs properly and her eyes didn't focus but I was
not prepared to face such profound disability and dismissed it as a
"newborn syndrome." It seemed so wrong that an innocent little
baby should be so handicapped. I refused to recognize the obvious.

As a parent, I was angry. Surely, the doctors in their medical
wisdom could have done something to prevent this unfortunate
error. How could God allow such travesty when He had the power
to make her whole? It wasn't fair! She would never have the
opportunity to experience a normal life, to run and sing and go to
college and get a job and fall in love.

As time passed, I became aware of the collage of feelings that
parents of special needs children experience and developed
friendships through the years with many of these parents. Some say
they feel responsible, even though they recognize there was nothing
they could do to alter the events. Some feel cheated that their
offspring will never have the future that these parents hoped for
them. Others feel self conscious, even embarrassed, when they take
the child out into public and the public doesn't understand or makes
curious, hurtful remarks.

Kathy was beautiful, with lovely blue eyes (that wandered at
will) and a soft, pink little body (that had no ability to move or sit or

41

do what normal little bodies do). After a few months, she was ready for solid food, which she quickly grew to love but had no ability to swallow. I seemed to innately know what to do and would massage her throat to assist the movement of food. To help her eliminate her bowels, I bent her knees to her chest and carefully moved them toward her body.

Despite the fact that she could not roll over or sit or develop her muscles normally, she was a sweet, happy baby and we loved having this precious little person in our family. Five year old Diane was gentle with Kathy and spent hours talking and touching and singing to her.

While Kathy was with us, we moved to acreage on the outskirts of town. There, Dave and I built a house "from scratch." Everything from pouring the concrete foundation piers to laying the roof. Our temporary home was a 35 foot trailer parked near our building site. It was cramped and I worried that the Agency might remove Kathy because of the small living quarters but they assured us that having her in a loving, caring family was more important than a fancy house and they could see that our living conditions were clean and safe. That did not alter the fact that it was small. The girls slept in the bedroom while Dave and I used the living room couch.

On warm days, I often put Kathy outside in the playpen where Mitzi would sit at attention nearby and keep her good company. The dog seemed to sense that this special child was unable to care for herself and protected her like a dedicated body guard.

Months passed. Then, a year. Diane started kindergarten and I was pleased to have Kathy's company. I instinctively understood her needs and her special care became routine.

When the social worker called, it took me by surprise because I was not expecting to hear from her for some time. She said that they were coming to remove Kathy from our home in a few days because I was giving her what they considered 24 hr. nursing care and I was not a nurse. I could not argue that point but we had all become so attached to this little darling and I felt we were doing a good job with her care. Again, it was time to endure the painful agony of losing someone we had grown to love.

I wanted to have Kathy baptized but had no legal right to do so. I baptized her myself, in the kitchen sink, sprinkling her head with a few drops of water, dedicating this special little person to God. I wept as I held the limp little body against my own and felt my tears mingling with the water in my hand.

Unlike our separation from Ricky and Maryann, the social worker we had for Kathy readily shared information about her move. "She will be living in a care home, operated by a registered nurse," the social worker said. "It accommodates several physically and mentally handicapped children." Diane was at school the morning the social worker picked up Kathy and her worldly goods. I waved goodbye to a little girl who couldn't wave back, but there is no doubt she understood my kiss on her forehead, just before she was placed in the car.

The day after she left, I found some clothes I had forgotten to send along so I called and was given permission to bring them to the care home. Excitedly I drove over, fully expecting to see how Kathy was adjusting to her move and new surroundings but they would not let me see her. The care giver was patient with me as I ran my hands over the little dresses I brought and fought back the tears.

She appeared to be short handed and overworked and, although she didn't rush me, I sensed that she had little extra time for anyone and the sooner I left, the sooner she could get back to her harried schedule. I wondered if the children there were being physically cared for but emotionally deprived because the workers had little time for individual attention.

In the weeks that followed, we received periodic reports about Kathy but they were discouraging. The Agency had traded quality care in a loving home for care in an overpopulated, under staffed, facility because it met a criteria in their book of rules. Within three months, Kathy was dead.

44

Mary

Dave and I did our best to overcome the loss of Kathy by working long hours on the house. Diane pitched in where she could and we began installing the insulation. In the meantime, we acquired a baby goat that Diane named Mary.

Why the little goat came to us before she was weaned, I cannot remember but will say she came to the right place because Mitzi had a new litter of puppies and an abundance of milk so she took on Mary, also, and nursed her until she was ready for solid food.

Apparently, the goat food we furnished was not to her liking because Mary began chewing on the fiberglass insulation we had just installed. Then, she turned mean. Could it have been the diet?

One day, she kicked me and it hurt and I complained to Dave who laughed it off. The next day, she kicked Dave and it wasn't quite as funny so he gave Mary to a farmer friend, hoping she would have a better life where she had more freedom.

A few weeks later, Dave saw the farmer at the feed store. "How was Mary?" he inquired. "Delicious!" the farmer replied.

The Four Day Baby

The new house was not ready for a move but we couldn't wait so, while there was no finished paint on the inside walls and we were walking on sub-flooring, we moved in. Compared to the small trailer, this was spacious living!

The floor plan had two bedrooms and a bath on one side and a large open area on the other side. A work island separated the living room from the kitchen, with a dining area at one end of the room. We were surrounded by windows, with future plans for a deck in the back. Once settled, I called the Agency and said we were ready for another child.

It was summertime and I had flannel boards and curriculum and peppy song sheets spread out on the living room floor in preparation for Vacation Bible School the following week. I should have known better than to contact the Agency when I did because so many foster children were waiting to be placed, it took but a few days for that phone to ring with a rather urgent plea. "We have a little eleven month old girl here named Julie."

I told her we had just had a foster baby and would prefer someone older who could play with Diane. The worker assured me that this was short-term. "We are trying to reach relatives in Oregon and wonder if you would be willing to take the child for four days which should give us enough time to reach them and get her placed." "What's four days?" I thought. "No problem."

On Friday, the social worker and Julie's mother delivered the little spitfire. Julie's mother was mentally ill and needed hospitalization. In her pockets were dried bread and raw wieners which apparently had been Julie's diet, along with milk. I believe the mother wanted to be a good care giver but her own needs were overwhelming so she sought help through foster care without consulting Julie's father. Perhaps, in her mental condition, she did not trust the father to care for Julie.

Here was the most active child I had ever seen. Not yet able to walk, she moved across the room like a lizard. Diaper changing was a challenge because she couldn't lay still. These were the days

47

before disposable diapers and the cloth ones needed to be pinned. I learned to work fast and, once done, did not need to pick her up for Julie would roll over on the bed and scoot herself off onto the floor. This kid was FAST!

We managed to get to Bible School on Monday, with guitar slung over one arm and Julie slung under the other. Diane wrestled the flannel board, which was almost her size, and the many characters that would be used for stories. Julie, not willing or able to sit still, kept me running constantly and I was becoming exhausted but took comfort in remembering this would only last four days. God had other plans.

On the second day, her father came for a visit. I felt sorry for him because he seemed lost in this experience. Apparently, he had been her primary care giver and was upset that his wife, needing hospitalization for a mental condition, put their child into foster care. For the time being, this seemed to be the best plan, however, because his wife had incurred so many bills, he had to give up their apartment and would be living in his car while working to pay off the debts. We assured him we would cooperate in every possible way, hoping to relieve his concern.

Four days passed and we didn't hear from the Agency. When I called, they said there was some delay but they were still working on the move. Julie's dad came to pick her up for a weekend with his parents. I bought a new outfit for her with green overalls that had the words, "I'm going to Grandma & Grandpa's" embroidered on the bib. Her grandma told me later that they were very anxious about Julie having been placed in foster care until they saw the overalls and felt relieved and that everything would be all right.

Grandma called Julie "Joanne's Missionary Project." We developed a friendship that continued to flourish over the years.

Testing My Strength

When Julie began to walk, she began to run. In a short time, she learned to climb, bringing the entire neighborhood to its knees in fear. When she called out, "Look at me," we looked UP. If she wasn't in a tree, she was balancing on scaffolding like a tightrope walker. This child knew no fear and disregarded good judgement which, in later years, resulted in a variety of scrapes, scratches, sprains, breaks, and concussions.

Because she admitted herself to the mental hospital, Julie's mother had the right to take herself out at any time and she exercised that right in short order. Within a couple of weeks, she was back living with a variety of people she had just met.

She had no personal friends because she was new to the area but very cleverly talked herself into relationships with people she met at the health clinic or a church or a store and that is how she found a place to stay. One after another felt sorry for her and took her in, only to be confronted with this complex personality that was so abnormal, they couldn't cope with it. Then she moved on to the next place.

The court had awarded her the right to take Julie every other weekend and someone different drove her out to our home almost every visit. It was a horrible experience for me because, possibly in her desire to have Julie with her permanently, the mother told her she was keeping her and not taking her back to our home. Here was a little preschooler who didn't know where she was or how to return to us, staying with a mentally unbalanced mother who had new friends and a different place to stay almost every time she took the child away.

When she was less than three years old, and her mother appeared at the door, Julie would run the length of the livingroom and smash herself against the wall, as if to harm herself. As clean and well dressed as Julie was for the visit, her mother undressed and bathed her in our tub before taking her out. She also sang to my husband who was at a loss to know how to respond.

49

Neither Dave nor I were educated about severe abnormal behavior and we both felt uncomfortably helpless. Fortunately, the Agency was aware of this and provided us with a psychiatric social worker who helped to interpret the mother's actions and was available to us by phone whenever we needed help.

We told Julie how much we loved her and demonstrated it in many wonderful ways. Then, every other weekend, we let a mentally ill person, who frightened her terribly, pick her up from our home and take her away to strangers in strange places.

Julie didn't understand that we had no choice about this court order. All she knew was what happened and I cannot imagine the fears she dealt with or the feelings of betrayal and abandonment by our family that she must have felt. There was no place to run, no where to feel safe. As she got older, and her mother called on the telephone, Julie got such earaches that we would rush her to the emergency room only to find that her ears were healthy but her emotions were bleeding .

Panic overtook me when Julie's mother went to court and filed for custody. We gladly testified on behalf of the father but neither Dave nor I had been on a witness stand before and we had no idea how bitter and ruthless an opposing attorney could be.

The session took several hours, during which I continuously prayed and watched the face of the judge. He intently observed the mother as she testified, so cleverly, so deceivingly, and I wondered if he could see through that. My hope was that we were dealing with a Solomon who would make a wise judgement. We were. His decision was to leave Julie in the custody of her father and in our foster care for the time being. Her mother could file for custody again at a future date but we were free from that threat for a while.

The court appearance was over but my emotional trauma had just begun. That night, I had a fitful sleep and woke to find my pillow covered with blood. I had chewed all my fingernails down to the quick. My nerves were shattered. Appearing in court and having the possibility of losing Julie to a mentally deranged mother, who falsely accused me of child neglect, was more than I could handle.. I was exhausted and I was frightened. With the mother free to seek custody at some future date, I wondered if I had the strength to go through this again.

Is She Wired Or What?

With the custody battle behind us, we tried to return to some semblance of normalcy but "normal" no longer meant freedom from stress and worry. Julie's mother was still allowed to take her from our home and, as concerned as we were for this little girl's safety, all we could do was create the best possible home life when she was with us.

Although she was a handful, I adapted to her rapid pace and prayed daily for the energy to keep up, hoping the Agency would leave her with us. By now, the "four day baby" was such a part of our family, we couldn't imagine life without her. Words like "hyperactive" or "attention deficit disorder" had yet to be coined. We just knew we had an unusually active child who needed to be kept busy.

We moved farther out into the country where we had horses and miles of riding area. Julie became a good rider but always on the cutting edge of disaster. She was as adept bareback as with a saddle and one day I looked out the window to see her <u>standing</u> bareback as the horse patiently trotted along. She had seen it done on TV and wanted to try it out for herself.

In the wintertime, our school district provided bus transportation to a ski area where the students received a lesson, lift ticket, and full day of skiing for a modest fee. Julie took every lesson offered, then hopped the lift to the top of the hill and came roaring down as straight and as fast as the skis would take her, ignoring anything the instructor had taught her about technique or safety.

When I first began watching her, my heart jumped into my throat and I felt paralyzed with helpless fright. For my own survival and peace of mind, I realized I had to accept that she would either survive or succumb.

There were numerous trips to the Emergency Room. "Have you ever had her x-rayed here before?" the technician questioned. "Yesterday," I truthfully replied. Keeping a cast on her limbs was next to impossible. One broken ankle occurred the day we were to leave on a camping trip to the ocean.

The plaster cast from toes to knee was barely dry when we left the hospital with Julie hobbling on her rented crutches. We cautioned her to take good care of the crutches since they needed to be returned in the same good condition or we would have to pay an extra charge. The doctor's only instruction was to keep the leg elevated and not put any pressure on her foot until after our next appointment.

Diane was waiting for her in the camper of our pickup truck and we boosted Julie up, got the two girls settled at a table where they could play games while we traveled, and Dave and I simultaneously sighed a breath of relief as we slid into the cab of the pickup and drove off. We needed a little quiet time together and took advantage of the four hour drive.

It was dark when we arrived at the ocean. We backed into our designated parking spot near the water's edge, enjoyed a cup of hot chocolate, and bedded down for the night. I was exhausted and fell into a deep sleep that lasted for hours.

When I woke, everyone was still asleep except Julie who was gone. I parted the curtains and squinted at the bright early sun. There she was, running in the shallow water with her crutches in the air like a pair of wings. Quickly, I slipped into my clothes and ran out to the water's edge. When she saw me, she yelled out, "Don't worry, Mom, I'm keeping the crutches dry." It took three casts but the leg finally healed. We eventually invested in a pair of crutches we could call our own, once we realized they would be used on a rather regular basis.

Mrs. Henderson

Julie found school difficult, especially math. Sometimes, after supper, we remained at the table to play dice games with her so she could work with numbers in a relaxed surrounding. It wasn't until college (yes, we are talking about our four day baby here) that she was diagnosed with Dyslexia. It upset me to think of how she, how all of us, suffered through thirteen years of schooling and no one picked up on the possibility of her learning difficulty being the result of a disability. I can only be grateful it was finally discovered and given attention and help.

Mary Jane Henderson was Julie's third grade teacher. I believe she was an angel, sent to us as an encourager for our entire family. She seemed to have a divine understanding of this little girl and a practical solution to many of her problems.

Mrs. Henderson innately knew when Julie had been to visit her mother because her hyperactive behavior was out of control. She had little home spun solutions for those times, like saving the nubs of pencils that were not longer usable by the students. When Julie was impossible to work with, Mrs. Henderson gave her a box of the pencil nubs and told her to break them in half to get some of the frustration out. If Julie was disruptive to the class, Mrs. Henderson sent her outside with instructions to "kick a tree." It helped calm Julie down enough to return to class and function with the others.

Here was a teacher who recognized fear, anger, aggression, frustration, and tension and had the wisdom to deal with it intelligently. As much as I hated to lose the wonderful relationship we had developed with Mrs. Henderson, I imagined how relieved she must have been, at the end of the school year, not to have Julie in her class any more.

In August, information arrived from the school about the coming school year and it indicated that Julie was to have Mrs. Henderson for the fourth grade. I picked up the phone and made an immediate call to the school, where the teachers were preparing their rooms, and asked to speak to Mrs. Henderson. When she came to the phone I explained that we did not expect her to take

Julie again and understood perfectly if she wanted Julie transferred to another teacher. "I requested Julie again." she said. "I think she needs all the stability that we can give her."

I whispered, "Thanks," and hung up. There was no way to hold back the tears that poured down my face.

Can I Do This?

Other foster children joined our family while Julie remained. One day, the Agency called that they had a twelve year old girl named Candy who needed a home. She had some physical disabilities and was one of twelve children. As devoted as her mother was, she had her hands full with just the normal routine for such a large family.

Candy was being treated for Lupus in a children's hospital where she had been a patient for a year. She took a variety of medications, one of which caused deterioration in her spine so she wore a cumbersome metal brace on the front of her body, from neck to the pelvic area. The medicine also made her appear "puffy" and overweight. Her cheeks were so full, they pushed her eyes almost shut.

As an adult, I was extremely aware of Candy's appearance but it didn't seem to bother Diane or Julie. I picked her up at the hospital, several hours distance from our home, and when we finally arrived back at the house, Julie met us at the door. Her first words were, "We love you, Candy." What unconditional acceptance.

The counselor at Children's Hospital cautioned me that emotions had a lot to do with the illness and I should never use corporal punishment or allow Candy to get upset. It was an unreasonable request, we soon learned, but I was willing to do anything to encourage a healthy recovery. She required full time attention for several months and the other girls willingly took a back seat to those needs. I felt that I was slighting them but saw no way to balance my time.

I kept a list of the many medications and their instructions. Every few hours, I took Candy's brace off and exercised her legs and arms. With every lift, I prayed that God would strengthen them and return them to good health. It seemed unrealistic but Ricky had renewed my faith in the power of prayer and I remembered God's powerful answer. It happened then and could happen again.

Candy was behind a year in her school work and, because she was still too ill to study or concentrate for any length of time, the school district assigned her a home teacher who spent three morning hours with us each weekday.

The home teacher was a nervous little lady in her menopausal years who could no longer handle the stress of a classroom and told me she came close to a break down the day the kindergarten children tipped over the piano. I wondered how that could have happened but decided that asking would only add to the stress.

The teacher shuffled up to our door, books in hand, probably with the best intentions to plant a few new facts in Candy's mind but, the truth is that she spent more time talking to me than teaching Candy. Nevertheless, it seemed to be a good arrangement for both teacher and student, and I appreciated anything she taught Candy that might bring her up to grade level again.

As Candy developed a trust in me, she openly shared her feelings and fears. One day, when I was ironing, she sat at a nearby table and chatted, jumping from one topic to another. Some were serious and others were nonsense, and then she caught my attention.

She told how her father sexually molested her, and her sisters, and how frightened she was of him. "I used to lay there and wish I was a boy." she said. I froze in place and almost burned the piece under my iron. It was difficult to remain calm and continue to work when I was seething with anger inside.

Having had a similar, but not as serious, experience in my own childhood, I understood how helpless she felt and how haunted she was by the memory. I reported our conversation to the social worker who initiated an investigation and found that the father had, indeed, molested all the girls, including a three year old. It wasn't until one of the older sisters had enough courage to testify against him in court that he was jailed.

Expanding our Horizons

We were confined to home by Candy's illness but found ways to expand our horizons. Dave bought a used 16mm sound projector and I borrowed films from the library. Most of them were educational, some a little boring with a few cartoons available now and then but they were a novelty and we always learned something. To liven it up, we showed the films on Friday nights when the children could stay up later and we popped popcorn and made root beer floats. Sometimes, we invited neighbor children to join us and they all thought it was a real treat.

As Candy improved, we expanded our horizons to another level by purchasing a small used travel trailer and often spent weekends away from home, seeking out new places and new experiences.

The trailer was too small to accommodate a bathroom so we bought a porta-potty that could be emptied later. Unfortunately, it got tipped over one cold day when we were a good distance from home. The contents rolled into a floor vent that led directly to the heater below which was cranking away at full speed. What followed was a series of splashes, splats, steam, and odor that defies description. Dave's only remark was, "There must be a better way to clean out our sinuses."

Candy Improves

Ricky had been right. Prayer worked, along with lots of exercise and a decrease in medication. We were finally able to remove the cumbersome body brace and free Candy of that added weight and unsightly bulge under her clothing. It was the decrease in strong steroids that allowed her body to strengthen enough so that she could return to school and no longer need a home teacher. Her condition was still delicate enough to require transportation on a bus for the handicapped but, within a few months, that also was no longer necessary and she was able to ride the regular bus to school.

Eventually, she gained enough strength to participate in a P.E. class. Again, our entire family rejoiced with each new step toward normalcy but becoming normal and healthy was not easy for Candy. Since the onset of her illness, she had spent a year in the hospital and two years in our home, receiving a tremendous amount of personal attention. This became her comfort zone and being normal meant less attention, less control, and more sharing of my time with Diane and Julie.

"Discipline your son (daughter) in his (her)
early years while there is hope.
If you don't, you will ruin his (her) life"
(Proverbs 19:18).

Not being able to discipline Candy like the other children became a problem. I used every ounce of creative persuasion and reasoning within my ability but there was no doubt that I treated her differently from the other girls. She purposely "pushed my buttons" to force some kind of discipline.

Now that she was improved, I enjoyed giving Diane and Julie some personal one-on-one time which they deserved. Not once in the two years had either of them complained about being ignored when Candy was receiving so much attention. They could see, when she first came, how needy she was physically and they fell into the routine right along with me.

By the time I had met Candy's needs I was exhausted and, although the other girls didn't complain, I felt guilty. Now, it was payback time and I enjoyed sharing myself three ways for a change.

Candy rebelled and regressed physically just enough to, again, require the majority of my time. I was amazed at the control she had over her illness and discussed this with the social worker who assured me this is a technique often used under such circumstances. Along with this physical relapse, she also became increasingly disobedient.

"Enough is enough!" I said emphatically to Dave one evening after a particularly difficult encounter with Candy. "I can no longer go on this way and I cannot, in good conscience, allow Candy to become a social cripple because she is being treated like a hot house flower."

I called her out from her room, where she had gone to pout. "Candy," I said, "I was told by your care givers at the hospital not to spank you or upset you emotionally and I have tried for two years to do this to the best of my ability. You have become increasingly disobedient and I think it is only fair to you to discipline you as I would the other girls under the same circumstances. I may lose you but I feel responsible to be a good mother to you and I no longer can allow you to behave in this manner."

Ordinarily, one would not spank a fourteen year old but I felt it was the appropriate discipline for the circumstances so I gave her a couple of swats on the behind. She turned around and said, "What took you so long? I have been trying for two years to get you to treat me like the others." The next day, I reported the encounter by phone to the social worker who agreed that I had done the right thing. I never spanked Candy again but I did use more strict behavior than before and was less concerned about emotional reactions that would trigger an onset of her illness.

Candy's Abrupt Move

Dave enjoyed the children and was a helpful Dad when he was home but his work increasingly called him away, leaving me with the full responsibility. One evening, Candy and I were talking together about her difficulty sharing me with the other girls. Finally, she said, "If I killed you and me, we would be together in heaven, wouldn't we?" I was stunned and didn't believe for a minute that she would ever carry out such a plan but the statement made me feel uneasy and concerned for my safety and that of the other girls.

The next day, I reported the conversation to the social worker who decided it was time for Candy to return home now that she was healthy enough to care for most of her personal needs and would not require too much of her mother's attention. Her father was back in the home, under careful supervision, and no longer posed a threat to any of his daughters.

It was a sudden move, a surprise Candy never expected, and it had a profound effect on her, I learned later. She integrated back into her family although, when I called a few days later to see how things were going, her father said she came back pretty spoiled. I couldn't disagree with him because, with just our three girls at home, she got most of the attention for two years. Fortunately, it did not take her long to adjust back into her family of twelve children.

Candy went on to graduate from high school, marry, and raise two lovely children. We did not see or hear from her again for twenty years.

I answered the phone one day and recognized her voice immediately. Candy and her family were in the area and wanted to meet with us. Only Julie and I were available at the time so we hopped in the car and were off in a flash. "What would she look like after all these years?" I thought. She was probably thinking the same about me. "What will we talk about," I wondered. "Will she be angry with me?"

She looked much the same. In fact, younger than her 34 years. We met her husband, a tall, good looking gentleman, and her two children who were in their teens. After the usual pleasantries, Candy told me that she had felt betrayed by us because of the sudden move. Having felt betrayed once by my own mother when I was young, I embraced Candy and asked for her forgiveness, explaining that we did what the Agency thought best, for her and for us, at the time.

Our once fractured relationship became repaired and I appreciated Candy's openness to discuss her feelings after so many years. It was thrilling to see her again and meet her fine family. I was so proud of her, to have overcome many obstacles and gone on to live a productive life. She continues to battle Lupus and Rheumatoid Arthritis, plus a variety of personal issues but she has dealt with them intellectually as well as practically and is a genuine survivor.

The "Dull" Child

After the social worker took Candy back to her family, we chose to wait a while before bringing other foster children into our home.   Julie deserved extra attention and Diane had   some difficulty in school. Physically, she was often tired. Her left foot improved with the orthopedic shoe but her kidney continued to be a problem and she often wore a patch over her one eye.

By now, she was in the third grade and could not read well or do the simplest math problems without a struggle. Our educational reading program was in a transition with phonics being replaced by word association. Children looked at a picture and tried to guess what the word below it said.

The school Principal called me into his office one day for a conference. He stated that the school counselor and Diane's teacher had concluded she was a dull child.   I was shocked! I couldn't believe my ears! "What can we do to help her and help you?" I anxiously asked. "I suggest you just take her home and enjoy her." was his reply. Were we discussing the same child?

Admittedly, she was slow. I wasn't sure if this had anything to do with her physical health or her biological heritage or poor teaching or "all of the above" but the Principal seemed to be describing an unteachable child who would probably not progress far in the educational system, and certainly never graduate from high school.

Dave and I were more than offended by the Principal's suggestion. Diane needed extra attention scholastically but she was a cooperative student, never a discipline problem, and the thought of taking her home and just enjoying her was ridiculous.

I prayed anxiously for the next few weeks, hoping for a clue, some direction, but without much success. On the discouraging days, I began to doubt myself. Was Diane really more handicapped than I would admit? Was I in denial, like I had been with baby Kathy when she first arrived? Dave and I both saw hope and promise and possibility in Diane and we agreed that to allow her to stop learning at this age would be a gross disservice.

It was nearing the end of the school year so she continued in her class while I researched new avenues, beginning with private school. Across the street from our Presbyterian church was an Episcopal church that included a school with classes from kindergarten through eighth grade. I was pleased that she might attend a Christian school and felt confident that this was the answer so, late one afternoon, Diane and I visited the Principal.

For whatever reason, perhaps a difficult day, she was in a very bad mood and sounded angry when she spoke, telling Diane they had high standards and expected a great deal from their students. For those who did not comply, there was punishment. She said nothing complimentary about her teachers or students, the curriculum or extra-curricular activities. Every subject she covered was in a negative tone and she had Diane scared.

As cordially as possible, I ended the conversation and led Diane back to the car. We both just sat for a few minutes before I turned on the ignition. "Please, Mama, oh please," Diane pleaded, "don't make me go there. I'll study harder. I'll do anything." and the words faded into sobs. I took her hands in mine and made a promise. "You have nothing to worry about, my dear," I said, assuredly. " I feel the same way you do. That is not the school for you." We drove off and spoke little to each other on the way home.

What a disappointment the visit had been. That Principal had every opportunity to impress me, a paying parent, with the qualities of her school but she chose to vent her frustrations on us instead. I had never been involved with a Christian school and decided that, if this was any example, they could keep it.

We hired a tutor, a school teacher friend who loved children and loved teaching, who met weekly with Diane and gave her work to finish before the next week. Slowly, very slowly, the seeds of improvement were planted. Small, small seeds.

As the school year ended, we needed to make some arrangements for the following Fall. Diane's teacher and counselor both recommended that she repeat the third grade but they gave little hope for improvement.

Neither Dave nor I had a problem with holding her back but we both felt she should change schools to avoid the stigma of classmates moving on while she remained behind, and also to avoid having the same teacher.

> *"So be truly glad!*
> *There is wonderful joy ahead,*
> *even though the going is rough for a*
> *while down here"*
> *(1 Peter 1:6).*

I continued to pray for some direction, reminding the Lord and myself of how much we loved Diane. While browsing through the Weekly Shopper, a free newspaper that gave local news and grocery specials, a small article caught my eye. The headline read, "New Christian School to open in area," and gave a phone number for interested parents to call. That number turned out to be the answer to my prayer. St. Albans, also affiliated with the Episcopal Church, was celebrating its groundbreaking and planned to be open for the Fall semester. The monthly tuition, cost of supplies and uniforms, was within our budget.

Dave and I attended an informational meeting for parents and, from then on, I involved myself in every activity that would assure a Fall opening. The school budget did not include new plastic desks with free form molded legs. We were reduced to renovating old wooden desks with the hole for an ink well. It meant lots of "elbow grease," sanding and varnishing but the parents worked as a team and we got to the point where we looked forward to meeting and working and getting better acquainted.

The day the desks were completed, we celebrated with a picnic. Since no bus service to the school was going to be available, the parents arranged car pools which meant driving several miles each way, twice a day, but I didn't mind and sensed it was going to be a good year for the entire family.

About two weeks before opening day, the milkman who was to make daily deliveries made a dry run to the school so he would be familiar with directions. Seeing the amount of work that remained, he concluded that the school could not possibly open on the scheduled date and so he failed to deliver. After a call from the Principal, who let him know that we had a dedicated group of parents who saw that the school open on time, he faithfully delivered the milk every day.

Most of the children were new to each other, and Diane was not the only one repeating third grade, so school took on a new excitement. Private school was different, with class size about half that of public school and teachers who were dedicated to educational fundamentals.

Diane liked it and looked forward to going each day but it was a scholastic struggle. The first report card showed mostly Cs and Ds. At the top of the card, however, was a big "A" for character and citizenship. Tearfully, she tried to rationalize the poor grades for her determined efforts. As I held her close and dried the tears, I reassured her that those grades would improve in time. We already saw improvement. "Getting an 'A' in Character and Citizenship meant a lot," I told her. "Your teachers will help you accomplish better math and reading in time but being of good character and a good citizen is something special, a gift of God that comes from within." By now the tears were gone and she listened intently. "You reflect God's love in how you act toward, and take an interest in, other people. If you were going to get an 'A' in anything, I am glad it was in Character and Citizenship."

Diane barely squeaked through her second try at third grade. Had we remained at that school, there is a good possibility they would have had her repeat it again but, that summer, we moved several miles away to the country where there was no private school so we enrolled her in the fourth grade in public school.

She had learned so much in one year at St. Albans that keeping up with the rest of the class now was possible. Also, she had grown tall in the past couple years and remained the tallest child, boy or girl, until she reached the sixth grade. By that time, she matured scholastically to the point that, from then on, we couldn't hold her back.

In high school, Diane entered a contest, sponsored by the Odd Fellows and Rebecca Lodges, that gave the student who learned the most about the United Nations an opportunity to travel to the U.N. plus all the battlefields of the Civil War. She wrote papers, took tests, gave speeches, and saturated her mind with information, often starting her day at 3 AM and continuing until well past dark.

I became concerned that she was pushing herself too hard and told her she didn't have to do that for her Dad and me. We were satisfied with her progress and didn't expect more than she could comfortably give. She replied, "Mom, when I was young, you set my goals. Now that I am older, I am setting them and I don't want you to worry. I like the challenge." She won the trip and was selected to give a speech at the United Nations.

After high school, she worked for a couple of years and then entered college where she completed a five-year nursing program and received a Bachelor of Science in Nursing degree.

What if I had listened to that Principal back in the third grade? What if I had taken Diane home and "enjoyed" her, as he suggested? What if Dave and I had not given her the opportunity to improve. She may have become a social cripple, dependent upon us for her entire adult life. Instead, she struggled for a couple of years and then took off like a rocket, setting her sights on goals we never thought possible.

Although college was difficult, she became such a good student, some of her instructors encouraged her to continue studying for a Master's Degree, even a Doctorate, so she could become an instructor herself because she had such good, natural, teaching skills. By that time, however, she felt she had enough school for a while. Besides, she was in love. It was time to get married and begin a family of her own.

During her nursing career, Diane took special interest in children and became especially successful working in the Adolescent Oncology ward where she brought nursing expertise, sound common sense, and comforting Christian faith and hope to dying youngsters and their families.

Diane lives in Canada now. Her husband is pastor of a growing, young church and is studying for his doctorate degree Their oldest daughter spent a year in Finland as a Rotary Club exchange student and their next daughter went to Equador on the same program. At this writing, the family also includes a teen age son, an energetic eight year old son whom they adopted two years ago and a variety of foster children with severe medical needs. One teen age foster daughter has been a part of their family for several years.

Diane's nursing education and experience, along with the family working together to integrate these children's needs into their routine, has been successful and satisfying. They also have enjoyed opening their home to several foreign exchange students over the years.

Ole, Patrick and Lori

Reflecting back to those days in our country home, many foster children came and went. Babies, waiting to be adopted, had a short stay. Little Ole had blonde hair that was so thin it looked like down on a new chick. His nose was prominent and we hoped he would grow into it and not have it grow along with him.

Little Patrick came to us yellow with jaundice. His mother was a welfare recipient in another state where the rule was that, unless the newborn had a life threatening illness, it must be released from the hospital in two days. Since little yellow babies with malfunctioning livers were not the most desirable adoption candidates, he was placed with us until gaining normal, stable, health. At the time, Kerstin, a foreign exchange student from Sweden, was living with us for a year.

It was family policy to let Diane and Julie take turns naming newborns, just for the time they were with us, and this time we gave that honor to Kerstin. "What wonderful Swedish name would she choose?" we wondered. "Lars? Eric?" To say the least, we were surprised when she announced the baby would be called Patrick. So Irish!

One of our "waiting for adoption" babies provided us with not just joy and pleasure but a valuable lesson in life for Diane and Julie.

Lori came directly from the hospital. Her heritage was Oriental/Caucasian and she was the most unusually beautiful baby I had ever seen. Her parents were college students and very much in love but not married. Because of conflict in one of their families, and the knowledge that a mixed race child would not be accepted, they felt no alternative but to reluctantly release her for adoption. As the placement worker shared these strong feelings with us, I hoped that Diane and Julie would understand how difficult it was for some natural parents to give up their children for adoption but how they saw no other solution.

I remember Diane's questioning when she was about four years old. At night, I had a talk time with each child and Diane went through a period where she asked, "Why didn't my natural parents want me?" I quietly explained how they probably wanted her very much but, for some reason we do not know, they could not keep her so they made sure she had a loving family to care for her until she was grown up and could care for herself. She would kiss me and go to sleep. The next night, and the next night, and the next night we went through the same routine. "Why didn't they want me?"

I felt so inadequate and wondered where I was going wrong. Why couldn't she understand? The question finally was no longer asked but I felt that it was an unresolved issue that might never be answered to Diane's satisfaction. When the social worker told us about Lori, it was real. She had been there and told us, first hand, of the emotional suffering that went into this difficult decision.

Not just beautiful, Lori was the most intelligent baby I had ever been involved with. She had the ability to think and act far beyond her age and, consequently, was a very interesting child. Because she had everything going for her, beauty, brains, personality, we expected her to stay but a short time. However, she stayed on because the Agency wanted to find an Oriental or part Oriental family for her.

Finally, the social worker called that a couple had been selected and, if I wanted to, I could bring Lori down to the Agency instead of the worker driving out to pick her up. I quickly accepted, remembering the thrill, not just for me but for Diane's foster mother, when she lowered the precious baby into my arms.

I dressed Lori in a beautiful outfit and secured her in the car seat for the rather long drive to the Agency. On the way, I tried not to think of our prospective loss but about the joy we had shared. It was emotionally painful because, like all the other children we had fostered, we wanted to keep her forever. I parked the car and carried Lori up to the Agency office.

We waited outside the room where the worker and couple were talking and then came the magic moment when I was called to bring Lori in. She went willingly to the prospective father who held out his arms. He talked and cooed and made the usual silly noises we make to babies. The prospective mother was more reserved but

72

polite and spoke gently. After a comfortable length of time, the worker suggested I take Lori home and the couple could discuss their intent to adopt her and call the next day.

Our family was unusually somber that evening during supper, as we tried but failed at conversation. When I got Lori ready for bed, the girls didn't want me to put her down but played a long extra time, knowing they would never see her again after tomorrow. Dave was in denial. Lori totally won his heart and now it was breaking. The next day, Diane and Julie left for school with tears in their eyes.

I waited for a call from the Agency before dressing Lori for the trip downtown so that she would look fresh and clean for her new parents. The memory of Diane, at first sight, was still vivid in my mind. Her outfit was well used and often washed, fading the once vivid colors. On her feet were tiny hand knit booties with open toes. They were wool and had apparently been washed in hot water because they looked shrunken and tightly woven. It was not a Macy's wardrobe but could easily have been castoffs from a Thrift Store. Even then, I was asked to return everything upon the social worker's next visit. I bought a beautiful pair of new booties and asked to keep the worn ones as a reminder of that special day. The Agency agreed.

Now, it was important to me that Lori's new family not find her in rags but new, colorful clothing to keep as a joyous reminder. By noon, she was still in her sleeper and I hadn't accomplished a thing, waiting for the call.

It came soon after lunch and, to my total disbelief, the social worker said that the prospective mother became so nervous, she backed out. I was shocked! Our family would have given anything to adopt her and I simply couldn't understand anyone turning down this very special child. The social worker assured me that this was not unusual and there were other couples waiting. She would call me again when they had decided on the best home for Lori.

There was unbelievable screaming and jumping and delight when Diane and Julie dragged in slowly from school and saw Lori waiting for them. They hugged and kissed her and me and each other and her again. To them, this was a miracle. Dave was

73

shocked when he got home from work and there sat the little girl he had mourned over all day. Having her back was bittersweet for him because it meant going through the separation again.

About a month later, I got a call from the social worker to bring Lori down to be introduced to another couple. "This *has* to be it," I thought. "No baby as special as Lori should be turned down even once and it certainly can't happen twice."

Once again, dressed like a doll, she sat up alert in the car seat and watched the scenery go by as we drove to the Agency. The second couple was cordial and Lori seemed comfortable with them. Once again, I was instructed to take her home, giving the couple overnight to make a decision, with intentions to bring her back the next day.

When the social worker called the next morning, to announce that they, too, decided not to adopt Lori, I called Dave at work. "What is going on?" I questioned, and he was at a loss for answers but agreed that we should let the Agency know of our desire to adopt Lori. We knew the rules. They had been drilled into us in no uncertain terms but there was no choice. This seemed to possibly be God's will for our family and we needed to take the chance.

I called the social worker. She was not surprised to hear me say we were interested in adopting Lori. "We are still in the process of searching for an Oriental family," she said, "but, if an appropriate family does not surface soon, we will consider your request." I thanked God for the possibility and tried hard not to get enthused but that was not easy.

Several weeks passed and I felt that the more time gone by, the greater possibility that Lori might truly become a permanent part of our family. Then came the dreaded phone call. "We have found a family in Indiana and offered Lori to them for adoption," the social worker said. "The mother will be flying out on Thursday so have Lori ready to leave that day."

It was difficult to understand why the Agency went to so much trouble, finding a family from out of state when we were right here and wanted her so badly but I knew they were making every effort to place her with an Oriental family so her ethnic needs would be more realistically met. Still, it was painful.

74

"Oh, for wings like a dove, to fly away and rest!
I would fly to the far off deserts and stay there.
I would flee to some refuge from all this storm"
(Psalms 55:6-8).

I held tightly to the little girl and wanted desperately to run and hide. The social worker's car approached our house and I saw the prospective new adoptive mother get out. I clutched Lori and prayed, trusting that God had a plan for her and a plan for our family. It became clear, early in my fostering career, that God was using me in a special way in the lives of many children. I knew that my role was to give Lori a good, safe beginning, to love her deeply and enjoy her daily, not knowing which day might be the last.

The prospective mother had other children, waiting for their new sister, back in Indiana. I wanted to not like her, to find some fault, but she was a lovely woman, warm and intelligent, and she took to Lori from the get-go. They bonded right there in my livingroom and I had to admit that this was probably the best of the three placements and Lori was lucky it worked out this way.

Again, Diane and Julie saw how painful it was to give up a child and I hoped they would relate that knowledge to their own circumstances and recognize that someone who loved them made the same difficult decisions when they were babies.

Each loss of a foster child was followed by a period of mourning but we grieved Lori longer than the others because there was that thin thread of hope that we might get to keep her. Shortly before she left us, I had her picture taken at a studio. She was very photogenic and wore a white bonnet with a floppy lid and a daisy on the side. The pictures arrived after she was gone and I slipped them into a drawer for several weeks. Dave's wounds needed to heal enough for him to focus on the memories, not the loss.

Even Better Than Us

Dixie, age five, and her three year old sister, Missie, had been removed from their home because of abuse and came to us until they could be adopted. This would take time because Dixie was seriously wounded psychologically and needed extensive therapy. She was five years old and could not speak and had no control over her bowels or bladder. I shuddered at the thought of what her life had been like.

Missie appeared stronger, probably because she had not been exposed to such severe and painful abuse. Perhaps she was a favored child. She was blonde, chunky, and spunky. Dixie, on the other hand, was tall for her age and very thin. She had an angry nature and was vindictive toward her sister, always trying to harm her. One day, shortly after they arrived, Dixie pushed Missie into our swimming pool, fully clothed, and would possibly have ignored her if I was not near enough to rescue her.

The first night of their stay, I undressed Dixie and was preparing to change her diaper as she lay on the carpet. Diapering a tall five year old child seemed unnatural. Although she could not speak as we do, she communicated in a way I understood and it was as I pushed the pin through the diaper (before disposables) that she squirmed in helpless terror and said, "Don't poke me with the pin. My mommy hurts me with the pin."

I was careful from then on to never accidently poke her. Perhaps her mother did it as punishment or to vent anger that the child was not toilet trained, not accepting the fact that she was probably responsible for the problem.

As I prepared to help Dixie with her pajama top, I noticed bruises on the inside of her arm at the bend of the elbow and when I pointed to them, Dixie said her mother used to put the "medicine" there. Apparently, she injected the child with street drugs. A friend, who worked in Early Childhood Development for the County at that time, told me that some parents on drugs gave them to their children at adult parties and then watched their uncontrollable behavior as entertainment.

There were also many circular scars on Dixie's chest and back which our pediatrician recognized as cigarette burns. No wonder this child was troubled! She had lived a hell that we cannot comprehend. No wonder she couldn't speak and wasn't toilet trained. No wonder she was angry and vindictive toward her sister. She needed to take it out on someone. How she survived at all was a mystery.

Dave and I did all we knew how to make the girls feel loved and safe in our home but Dixie was almost beyond reach psychologically. She did not know how to be happy. All joy had been stripped away, leaving her a miserable little human being. I worried about the children moving from our home but knew we were not prepared to keep them on a permanent basis because we had problems of our own lurking in the future.

Dave needed open heart surgery. The responsibility of additional children could not even be considered, but who would take these two? I pondered this issue well into the night on many occasions wondering how anyone could handle Dixie without abusing her because she was such a difficult child. I seemed to think that no one would treat Dixie as kindly as we did. Missie would make any family happy but Dixie might be so harmful she would cause their new adoptive parents to spend the bulk of their time keeping the girls apart. "God," I prayed, "please allow these girls to be adopted by patient people." As if I needed to tell God what was best.

On one of her routine visits, the social worker shared that things were finally falling into place for the girls. I was eager to hear more. "Most of the time we make every effort to adopt siblings together," she said, "but in this case, we feel both girls will do better if they are adopted separately." What a brilliant decision! Finding a family for Missie would be no trouble. She was a very appealing child; cute, sweet, vivacious, inquisitive, and loving. Dixie, on the other hand, had none of these qualities and was not desirable adoptive material. She would require a very special, understanding, family.

In a matter of months, the Agency did find homes and made arrangements for the girls to leave in the same week. Missie, all smiles with a teddy bear tucked under her arm, went off with the social worker to her new family who lived about two hundred miles away. Dixie, on the other hand, remained at our house while her new family came daily to visit. Perhaps this was the wisdom of the social services, but it may have been God's way of showing me that there were other people in this world who could do what I was doing.

"And so it is with prayer - keep on asking
and you will keep on getting....."
(Luke 11:9a).

Her prospective mother and father were older than Dave and I. They had financial resources to offer extensive therapy for Dixie and had already made arrangements for counseling. THEY WERE PERFECT! Better than anything I could have imagined or planned. Maybe even better than we were.

I marveled at God's wisdom and compassion. Why this little girl had been allowed to suffer such pain and torture, I cannot say, but I saw now that she was being rescued and, hopefully, rehabilitated to some degree of normalcy. These new parents were taking on a gigantic task and would probably have moments of reflection, wondering if they made the right decision, but they appeared to be solid and strong. After a few days, Dixie went with them willingly and I can only pray that they lived happily ever after.

Barbie, the Wonder Girl!

Some foster children stayed a few weeks, some a few months, and some a few years but each one was special and, even when the stay was short, they made a lasting impression on our family.

One of our short-term visitors was Barbie, a vivacious, energetic, overly confident eight year old. The social worker stayed only a few minutes after getting Barbie settled in the room she was to share with Julie. Then, we took her on a tour of our house and acreage, with horses and a stream and lots of "great for climbing" trees.

The house was "U" shaped with a swimming pool in the center. Barbie chatted about herself every inch of the way as we toured from room to room, place to place. She had wild tales to tell and an imagination on overdrive. As we approached the pool, I asked her if she could swim. "I can swim and I can ride a motorcycle and I've picked up a rattlesnake," she said.

Without further comment, she literally walked into the swimming pool, clothes and all. I was shocked because she had moved so fast. As I waited for her to show me her best stroke, it was apparent she had none. She made no attempt to swim but held her arms and legs straight and stiff and sank to the bottom of the pool. "How did she do that?" I thought. "Why isn't she floating?" There wasn't a moment for more questions. Barbie lay, face down, on the bottom of the pool.

In I went, with no time to even slip off my new Hushpuppies. "Why couldn't I have been wearing rubber thongs?" I thought as I made my way to the bottom of the pool and grabbed the child. Up we rose and, upon reaching fresh air, she sputtered and coughed as she looked at me through wet eyes. "It's a good thing you came," she said, "It was dark down there." I asked her why she plunged into the water when she didn't have a clue how to swim. She didn't know but was sure I would come and get her.

I called Dave to announce the mermaid's arrival. "Don't let her on a horse," he said.

81

Did Someone Say
Four Day Baby?

Julie, our "four day baby," remained as these children came and went. As much as she was part of our family, the nagging truth was that each day together might be the last. How we loved this little tomboy who only wore dresses when absolutely necessary. She was the blue jeans kid who loved to be outdoors or with animals or working with Dave. They made a good team, regardless of the circumstances or project. Julie learned to cut trees and fish and repair almost anything in their garage workshop. She was Dave's shadow.

As much as Julie enjoyed going to grandma and grandpa's with her dad, the visits with her mother continued to agonize her and, by the time she was eight years old, patterns of behavior indicated a troubled child. We felt helpless, with no legal authority to change these visitations. Julie showed subtle ways that she wanted to be part of our family. At school, she wrote our last name on her papers.

Something had to be done. I could no longer stand by and watch this child suffer so I suggested to Dave that we approach the Agency about legally adopting her. He reminded me of the stern lecture I received, years ago, but I felt compelled to buck the system.

"Yes, be bold and strong!
Banish fear and doubt!
For remember, the Lord your God is with you
wherever you go"
(Joshua 1:9).

For days, I prayed that God would give me wisdom and the right words to present this situation to the Agency. Teachers and counselors at school gave me helpful information. The social worker welcomed me into her office and listened intently. "Julie

83

appears to be headed for turmoil in her teens," I said, "and if she doesn't have more stability at home than we can give her under the present circumstances, Dave and I both fear for her future."

Now that I was in it this far, it wasn't hard to boldly continue, "We love Julie and would like to pursue adopting her." I waited for the expected reprimand and being reminded of "policy," but was pleasantly surprised that the social worker agreed with me and said that they had made the same observations and came to the same conclusion. "First," she said, "you need permission from both of Julie's parents, and that won't be easy. It might be impossible."

Julie's father would be no problem, I reasoned, because we had integrated him into our own family as much as possible over the years and had developed a trusting relationship. Her mother would be the obstacle and our job was to convince her that this was best for Julie. Without her consent, no adoption could take place. I had it all figured out. In reality, it was exactly the opposite.

Since I had concluded that the mother was the barrier, it seemed reasonable to contact her first. Without her consent, there would be no need to even mention it to Julie's father. Her mother had remarried so we invited both she and her husband over one evening and arranged for the girls to be gone.

Dave explained our observations about Julie's behavior and that the school and Agency concurred. We reminded her of how much we loved Julie and presented our desire to adopt her and give her the permanency she so desperately needed. I tried to remain calm but my heart was racing. To our complete surprise, both Julie's mother and her husband agreed with us and said they had even discussed such a possibility between themselves. With only the slightest hesitation, her mother agreed to allow the adoption.

With that great hurdle behind us, we confidently contacted Julie's father and presented our case. "Absolutely not!" he replied. I couldn't believe my ears. How could he possibly refuse such a selfless offer after all the years we had included Julie in our family? "This is her golden opportunity," I thought, "having a permanent home, equal inheritance as one of our children, everything we can offer her as parents." My self-conversation was interrupted. "I am afraid to let you adopt Julie," her father said, "because I might lose her and not be able to see her any more." We assured him this would not happen and reminded him of our trust in him over these past years. "Now," we told him, "it is your turn to trust us." We explained that adopting Julie simply validated that she had a permanent home. He was, and would always be, her father and we assured him that his involvement in our family would not change. He agreed to think about it. We waited and then we waited some more. Days went by, then a week, then another week and, finally, the answer came. He agreed to the adoption.

They said it couldn't be done and we did it! We adopted a foster child! Today, it is commonplace but at that time it was almost always denied. One wonderful summer day, when Julie was nine years old, we drove to the judge's office in a room at our local fair grounds and Julie legally became our daughter.

When we left, she appeared disappointed and we asked what was the matter. "I thought it would be more exciting." she said. " I thought my mother and father would be here and we'd all go out to dinner or something." Little did she know the profound significance that brief meeting with the judge would have on her future. She spent the night with friends at a slumber party, and they celebrated the momentous occasion in their own nine year old way.

We welcomed her mother to visit our home at any time but she could not take Julie away. She rarely made any contact and later moved out of the area. Julie's father remained a good friend to our family. The adoption was no cure-all. There were years of difficulty ahead and he shared some of that with us. Julie remained especially close to her widowed grandmother and, as an adult, was instrumental in getting her the care needed when she no longer could remain at home alone.

The "terrible two's" were challenging but the "terrible teens" were especially difficult for our family. Although our four day baby had found a permanent home, she wanted to be grown up and independent long before she was ready and became a classic rebellious teen.

We were all miserable and there was a time when I felt that Satan, himself, was pulling on Julie's shirt tail. She had difficulty feeling secure, always wondering if she would lose those closest to her. Then, early in her twenties and in God's perfect timing, He revealed His power to intercede and change a heart. God spoke to Julie in a special way, with the promise that *He* would never leave her, and she made a 180 degree turnaround, becoming an enthusiastic Christian, leaning on God's wisdom for strength and direction.

Slowly, but deliberately, she made decisions for her future, the first being to enroll in a local community college where she earned an AA degree in Criminal Justice. Being a self-described "action person," she works in a maximum security prison as a correctional officer.

In college, she learned American Sign Language which allows her to converse with hearing impaired persons and do informal interpreting for deaf prisoners. Some day, she would like to remain at home and foster hearing impaired children.

In her late 20s, Julie married and had two sons. When she announced her first pregnancy, I pondered how she would ever handle children because she appeared to not have an ounce of patience. She hates to drive in traffic, abhors lines at the supermarket, and generally gets upset when things don't move along according to her schedule. What kind of a mother would she be? To my delight, she has more patience with her boys than most parents. It is remarkable and I am so very grateful.

They seem to have inherited her busy, active, energetic genes but there is medication now to help calm them down while, when Julie was young, we had no choice but to keep her busy. "Hyperactivity" and "ADD" now are commonplace and the behavior is better understood.

I am very proud of Julie. She is a genuine survivor, and such an example to others who have endured difficult circumstances. Her own life experiences have equipped her to support and encourage others during their difficult times.

"In everything you do, put God first,
and he will direct you and
crown your efforts with success"
(Proverbs 3:6).

The purpose of this book is not to encourage any one to adopt or foster children. It is to help anyone, who is struggling with seemingly unbearable circumstances or unsolvable problems, to look beyond their own strength and learn to lean on the wisdom of the Lord and trust Him. It is simply the story of God's faithfulness to me, even when I felt abandoned and betrayed. Hopefully, these scriptures will be helpful.

Life is challenging. We want to give up but know we can't. What we really want is the full picture, to be able to look ahead and know everything is going to come out as it should but what God promises us is to lead us, one step at a time. In reality, that is all we need to not only survive but to succeed. The Bible is a guidebook for our journey through life, as accurate as any map.

Reflecting on those first twenty years of marriage, I marvel at God's plan which was beyond anything I could have invented for myself. It required courage I didn't know I had. Because I felt bound by what I considered my limitations, it blew my mind to find I could surge so far beyond them when I had the faith to trust in God's direction. It was like being let out of a little box into a big world that was mine to explore. As a result, I lived a more exciting and interesting life than I ever could have planned for myself. Had I been given the smallest glance into the long-range future, I would have crumbled under the emotional pressure. Had I been in control, I would have taken the easiest, most comfortable way out and lived a safe but uninteresting life. Instead, God took me on a roller coaster of experiences that required courage and patience only He could give. My future was safely in His hands.

Some experiences related here involve loss; loss of the joy of bearing a child, loss of foster children as they moved out of our home and our lives. Kathy's death. I learned how to face grief and work through pain, finally accepting loss so I could move on. Only

God knew that those experiences prepared me for ones to follow, years later, when I worked in a Hospice.

As I interacted with terminally ill patients, I felt equipped to understand and relate to their feelings of loss and fear and helplessness. I also could offer them hope, having learned through my own experiences that we never give up hope because God's promises are sufficient to keep us going. As He promised Julie, "*I will never leave you.*"

Many children have called me "Mother." When I receive letters from Sweden, they begin, "Dear Mom." Children I helped raise, whom I no longer see or know their whereabouts, called me "Mama." Our home was a haven for friends of Diane and Julie, some of whom had a difficult family life. There was always a bed, popcorn, lots of laughter, hugs, and prayer for these girls who still call me "Mom." I am blessed. To think that an even dozen children sounded like total madness, and it was only the beginning .

My original definition of a mother is not who I am today. It is much broader and involves more than only our family. As much as I would like to have had the joy of bearing a child, I couldn't possibly love a child from my own womb more than I have loved those children loaned to me, and they are not all recorded here. Two of the most important children, and friends, in my life came along later but that's another story

"How thankful I am to
Christ Jesus our Lord
for choosing me as one of
his messengers,
and giving me the strength to
be faithful to him"
(1 Timothy 1:12).

EPILOGUE

The following is a Mother's Day card I received some years ago - the kind we call a "keeper."

Mom,

I remember:

My nightmares where you chased away my hurt and confusion about being adopted and how you made me feel <u>soooo</u> special.

The many days and nights that you cared for my sicknesses.

My fantastic party at Fairytale Town.

The times you took my dear friends, the McKnights, to the Music Circus and Disneyland.

Your "open home" policy to all my friends.

Your encouragement when you would say that "God has a special plan for your life, Diane." And most of all, your unfailing love. You didn't have to take me into your heart, but you did.

You are indeed wonderful! Thank you for all you have done in the past and continue to do today. You are the <u>BEST</u> mom in the world and I thank God for you every day.

It's only by your example that I am able to nurture and love these little ones of mine. I have learned so much from you I can't even express it. Thanks, mom. You have made my life a wonderful and fulfilling experience. I thank God that you picked me! I praise Him that He provided for me such an encouraging mother!

When I think of what my life would be like without you, I picture a lost little girl with no direction or purpose. Thanks for your investment in my life.

"Her children arise and call her blessed."
(Proverbs 31:28a).

Diane

That same year, the following card arrived from Julie. She was still single. Since marriage and motherhood, the cards have become more introspective but she often buys two cards, one sentimental and one similar to the following:

I was hungry.....and thou fed me......

I was cold.....and thou clothed me.....

I was sick.....and thou healed me......

I was sad.....and thou didst dry my tears.....

I was oftentimes a real creepeth and thou didn't knocketh my blocketh off!

Thanks, Mom, for your listening ear.

Love,
Julie

90

Dedication

This book is dedicated to all the children who joined our family at one time or another. Whether your stay was short or long, whether you were mentioned in this book or not, you helped to make me a complete person.

I believe that our time together was special. I cannot help but believe that it was by God's design.

Although most of you had to leave, there will always be a place in my heart and memory for only you and I want you to know that I pray often for each of you by name.

Mom

"He gives children to the childless wife,
so that she becomes a happy mother.
Hallelujah! Praise the Lord."
(Psalms 113:9).

About The Author

Joanne Williams has had a variety of work published over the past twenty years. This includes a book, VOLUNTEERS ARE SPECIAL, and a monthly magazine column for Activities Personnel in long term health care, a curriculum, HELP! I'M LOSING CONTROL!, for training Hospice Volunteers, and a weekly newspaper column that is being compiled into a book for future publication. She currently serves as contributing editor for a trade magazine, ACTIVITIES, ADAPTATION, AND AGING.

Now in a second marriage, Joanne and her husband, Lowell, live in Idaho. They share a blended family of four children and eight grandchildren.